ADAPTED FOR SUCCESS

SHARKS
AND OTHER FISH

Andrew Solway

Heinemann
LIBRARY

www.heinemann.co.uk/library
Visit our website to find out more information about Heinemann Library books.

To order:
 Phone 44 (0) 1865 888066
Send a fax to 44 (0) 1865 314091
 Visit the Heinemann bookshop at www.heinemann.co.uk/library to browse our catalogue and order online.

First published in Great Britain by Heinemann Library, Halley Court, Jordan Hill, Oxford OX2 8EJ, part of Harcourt Education.
Heinemann is a registered trademark of Harcourt Education Ltd.

Editorial: Sarah Shannon and Lucy Beevor
Design: Richard Parker
Illustrations: Q2A Solutions
Picture Research: Mica Brancic and Susi Paz
Production: Chloe Bloom

Originated by Chroma Graphics (Overseas) Pte. Ltd.
Printed and bound in China by WKT Company Ltd.

10 digit ISBN 0 431 90664 5
13 digit ISBN 978 0 431 90664 5

11 10 09 08 07
10 9 8 7 6 5 4 3 2 1

British Library Cataloguing in Publication Data
Solway, Andrew
Sharks and other fish. – (Adapted for success)
597.3
A full catalogue record for this book is available from the British Library.

Acknowledgements
The publishers would like to thank the following for permission to reproduce photographs:
Corbis pp. 7, 32, pp. 8, 16 (Amos Nachoum), 37 (Ivor Fulcher), 18, 27, 38, 43 (Jeffrey L. Rotman), 15 (Kevin Fleming), 6 (Lawson Wood), 25 (Ralph A. Clevenger), 17, 41 (Stephen Frink); DK Images p. 24; Getty Images pp. 12, 30 (Digital Vision), 20, 40 (National Geographic), 21 (Taxi), 34 (The Image Bank/Michael Melford); Nature Picture Library p. 31 (Kim Taylor); NHPA pp. 29 (B Jones & M Shimlock), 35 (Ernie Janes); Oxford Scientific Films pp. 13 (Norbert Wu), 21; Science Photo Library pp. 19 (Alexis Rosenfeld), 11 (Eye of Science), 39 (Fred McConnaughey), 26 (Gregory Ochocki Productions/Eric Haucke), 36 (Paul Zahl), 9 (Richard Ellis), 23 (Rudiger Lehnen), 28 (Scubazoo/Matthew Oldfield), 42 (Sinclair Stammers), 14 (Tom McHugh).

Cover photograph of shark with mouth wide open showing his teeth reproduced with permission of Getty Images (The Image Bank/Romilly Lockyer).

The publishers would like to thank Ann Fullick for her assistance in the preparation of this book.

Every effort has been made to contact copyright holders of any material reproduced in this book. Any omissions will be rectified in subsequent printings if notice is given to the publishers.

Disclaimer
All the Internet addresses (URLs) given in this book were valid at the time of going to press. However, due to the dynamic nature of the Internet, some addresses may have changed or ceased to exist since publication. While the author and publishers regret any inconvenience this may cause readers, no responsibility for any such changes can be accepted by either the author or publishers.

Contents

Some words are shown in bold, **like this**. You can find out what they mean by looking in the glossary.

Successful fish

Sharks are probably the most successful fish in the ocean. There have been sharks in the sea for over 375 million years. Different shark **species** live in different **habitats** and have different ways of life. The sharks that are best-known are fast-moving, deadly **predators**.

When sharks first appeared, there was only one kind of shark. Today, there are over 350 different kinds of shark, and over 27,000 kinds of fish. Why are there so many different species now, and where did they all come from?

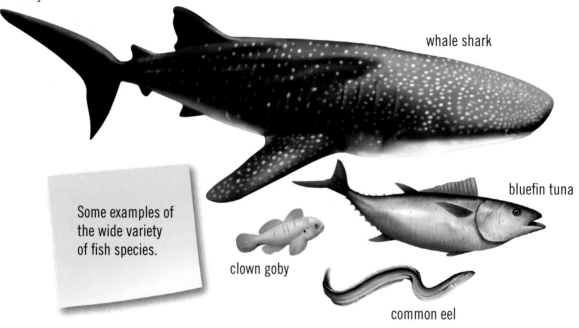

whale shark

bluefin tuna

Some examples of the wide variety of fish species.

clown goby

common eel

Fitting in

The ocean is not one uniform environment. Some parts of it are warm and light, while other parts are cold and dark. In some areas there is lots of food, while in other areas food is hard to find. No one species can survive in all of these different habitats.

As animals spread into new areas, or if their environment changes, they have to adapt to survive. An **adaptation** is a change that helps a living thing to fit into its environment. For instance, some sharks have adapted to living on the seabed by becoming flattened, so that they are hard to see.

Sharks and other fish have adapted to different environments and lifestyles in different parts of the ocean. The thousands of different kinds of fish we know today have **evolved** over millions of years and millions of adaptations.

WHAT IS A FISH?

Fish were the very first **vertebrates** (animals with backbones). Mammals, birds, and other vertebrates all evolved from fish. There is a huge variety of different fish, but they all have some basic things in common. All fish have a backbone and live in water although a few species, such as the mudskipper, can live on land for a time. Most fish have scaly bodies and they "breathe" water through pairs of **gills** on either side of the head.

Successful sharks?

How successful are sharks? There are several ways to measure the success of a group of living things. One way might be to say that if there are large numbers of a particular species, or group of species, then it is successful. However, a habitat can support many more small animals than large ones, so it is important to compare species of similar size.

Another measure of success might be the **range** of a species. This is a better measure, as it shows how adaptable a species is. Sharks have adapted to a wide range of ocean habitats, from shallow tropical seas to cold Arctic waters and the ocean deeps. By this measure of success sharks are very successful.

A third measure of success could be the length of time that a species or group has survived. On this measurement, sharks are among the most successful of all vertebrates as they have been around for over 375 million years.

Cladoselache was a very early shark from about 370 million years ago. Although it looked different from modern sharks, it was a high-speed predator.

How does adaptation work?

Evolution is the process by which life on Earth has developed and changed. Life first appeared on Earth 3.5 billion years ago. Since then, living things have evolved from simple single **cells** to the estimated 10 million or more different species on Earth today.

There are about 15 different angel shark species and all have flattened bodies and eyes on the top of their heads. These adaptations allow them to lie concealed on the seabed.

Useful changes

Adaptation is an important part of evolution. Being well adapted to its environment helps an animal or plant to survive and be successful. For instance, a tiger shark's saw-tooth teeth and powerful jaws are well adapted for its **scavenging** way of life (see page 19). Sea dragons, on the other hand, are amazingly well-adapted to hide themselves in their natural environment (see pages 24–25). How, then, does adaptation happen?

Variation

Not all individuals of the same species are exactly the same. You can see this yourself if you look around your class at school. Some people are taller than others; some people have fair hair while others have dark hair. Some people are musical, some are very clever, and some are good at sport. These differences between individuals of a species are known as **variations**.

Natural selection

The variation between individuals is what makes it possible for a species to change and adapt. The driving force for adaptation is called natural selection. Animals compete with each other for food, space, and for safe places to bring up their young. Individuals of the same species also compete with each other for the best **mates**. The animals that are best adapted to their environment survive and **reproduce**.

One recent example of natural selection is a group of fish in the Elizabeth River in Virginia, USA. The Elizabeth River is very polluted and most fish could not survive there. However, a species of small fish called killifish has adapted to life in these polluted waters. They can survive periods when there is hardly any oxygen in the water, and their bodies are very good at coping with toxic (poisonous) chemicals.

ALL IN THE GENES

Living things pass on characteristics to their offspring. A living thing's genetic material is a kind of "instruction book" for that individual.

Most animals and plants produce offspring by sexual reproduction. Males and females each produce special cells, known as **gametes**, which have only half the normal genes. Each parent provides half the genes for the offspring.

Cichlids are a group of about 2,000 fish species found in Africa and South America. They have elaborate courtship rituals that help females select a mate.

Sharks in their habitat

Different shark species are adapted for different kinds of habitat. Within a particular habitat, sharks live in different ways so that they are not in **direct competition** with each other.

Hammerhead sharks need to be agile to catch their favourite food – stingrays. A stingray has a powerful sting in its tail but this does not seem to bother hammerheads.

Shark shapes

What most people think of as the "typical" shark shape is a fish with a sharp snout and a long, streamlined body. This is the shape of a fast-moving shark, adapted to move quickly though the water. Predatory sharks need to be able to move fast to chase down their **prey**. Sharks with this "typical" shape live in various habitats such as in coastal waters, in deep water, and in the open ocean. Open ocean sharks, such as the mako and the blue shark, are the fastest swimmers.

Only some sharks have this typical shape. Some sharks that live on **coral reefs**, such as epaulette sharks or white-tip reef sharks, have long, thin bodies that allow them to hunt for prey in narrow cracks and gaps in the **coral**. Sharks that live on the sea bottom need to be able to swim close to the seabed. The bottom half of the body is usually flattened or the whole body may be flattened top to bottom, like the angel shark (see page 6).

The strangest-shaped sharks are probably the hammerhead sharks. Instead of a sharp, narrow snout they have a wide, flattened head. Although they are called hammerheads, the head looks more like a short wing than the head of a hammer. This wing shape makes hammerheads incredibly agile swimmers. They can make very tight twists and turns as they chase their prey.

DOWN IN THE DEPTHS

Some sharks live at great depths, where the water is always dark and very cold. The huge Greenland shark can grow to a length of 6.5 metres (21 feet) - about the length of a minibus! The Greenland shark lives mostly deep in the cold Arctic waters. It is slow-moving, but it still manages to catch fast-swimming prey such as squid, herring, and seals. It can live at depths of up to 2,000 metres (6,500 feet) where the **pressure** of water is 200 times that at the surface. However, these sharks also swim without problems in much shallower waters in the Arctic.

Greenland sharks are almost blind, and they have tiny, glow-in-the-dark **parasites** attached to their eyes. Scientists think that these parasites help to lure prey close to the shark's mouth.

Keeping warm

Most fish are cold-blooded. This does not mean that their blood is cold, but that they have no way of keeping their body warmer than their surroundings. Most sharks live in warm or cool seas. In colder waters their bodies begin to slow down, because the chemical reactions that produce energy in the muscles happen more slowly in the cold. This is not much good for a predator that needs to swim fast to catch its prey. However, the great white shark and some other types of shark have an adaptation that allows them to hunt in colder seas. Their blood system is designed so that warm blood coming from the centre of the body flows round the muscles. This helps to keep them warm when the surrounding water is cold. With warm muscles, the great white shark can swim fast even in chilly waters.

Sharks versus bony fish

In terms of numbers of species, sharks are in the minority in the oceans. There are about 370 species of shark and nearly 600 other species that are closely related. The rest of the 27,000 or so fish species are part of a different fish group altogether.

> The most important differences between sharks and bony fish are in their skeletons and the different ways they stay afloat.

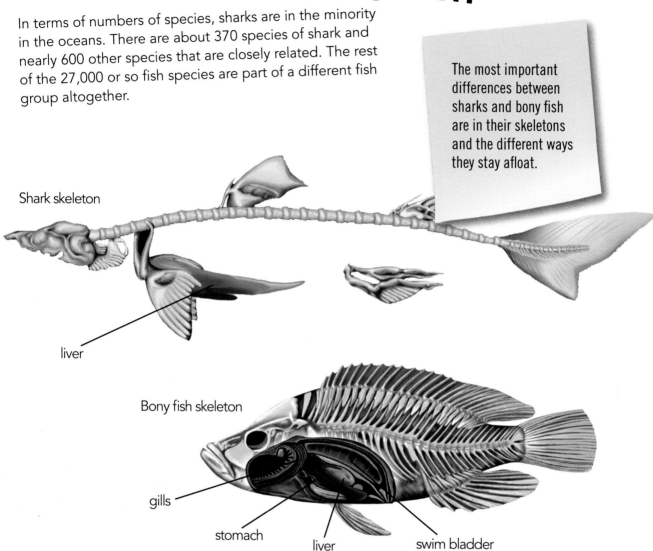

Shark skeleton

liver

Bony fish skeleton

gills

stomach

liver

swim bladder

Different skeletons

Sharks have very different skeletons from other fish. A shark's skeleton is not made of bone – it is made of a lighter, more springy material called **cartilage**. Sharks and their relatives, the skates and rays, are known as cartilaginous fish. The skeletons of other fish are made mostly of bone. This group is known as the bony fish.

The skeletons of both bony fish and sharks are heavier than the surrounding water. This means that they should have to swim quite hard all the time to avoid sinking. However, both groups have evolved adaptations to keep them afloat.

Keeping afloat

Bony fish can float comfortably at the depth they normally live at because they have a "balloon" full of gas inside their bodies, called a swim bladder.

A bony fish needs different amounts of gas in its swim bladder depending on depth. A fish at depth needs more gas than a fish near the surface, because as the fish swims deeper the swim bladder gets squashed by the pressure of water around it. The squashed-up gas in the swim bladder is less good at helping the fish to float, because it is more **dense**. When a bony fish wants to swim deeper it adds more gas to its swim bladder (it gets the gas from the sea). When a bony fish wants to rise closer to the surface it gets rid of some gas from the swim bladder.

The skeleton of a shark is lighter than that of a bony fish, but it is still heavier than the surrounding water. Sharks deal with this problem by having a liver that is full of oil. Oil is lighter than water so, overall, sharks are only slightly heavier than the surrounding ocean. If they stop swimming altogether they will slowly sink. Sharks must therefore swim to stay afloat, but they have the advantage that they can change depth more quickly than a bony fish – which must add or lose gas from its swim bladder. Sharks can move quickly from the surface to depths of hundreds of metres without any problem. Being able to change depth quickly gives sharks an advantage when they are hunting bony fish.

DIFFERENT SKIN

Another difference between sharks and bony fish is in their skin. Bony fish have flat, rounded scales that make the fish feel smooth to the touch. A shark's scales are much smaller, like triangular teeth. They are called **denticles**. The denticles make a shark's skin feel rough, like sandpaper. In fact shark skin, or "shagreen", was at one time used as sandpaper. This enlarged picture shows the tiny denticles that make up a shark's skin.

11

Where bony fish live

Like sharks, bony fish have adapted to live in all kinds of ocean environment, from the bottom of the deepest ocean to the shallowest shorelines.

Even this small area of coral reef shows a wide variety of corals and fish species. The most obvious fish in the picture are scalefins (orange fins) and yellow butterfly fish (flattened yellow and blue fish).

Coral reefs

Almost seventy per cent of all ocean fish species live in the warm, shallow waters around coral reefs. On a coral reef, competition for food and space is so fierce that many fish have become more **specialized**. Some fish live in cracks and spaces among the coral. Moray eels spend most of their lives in cracks in the rocks waiting for prey to swim past, and then they dart out and catch them.

Other fish are free-swimming and feed on the corals themselves, or the many small plants and animals that live alongside them. Parrotfish have horny "beaks" that they use to scrape up the plant-like **algae** that grow among the corals.

Some fish use the coral reef for shelter but feed away from the reef itself. Fusilier fish and creole fish both feed on clouds of tiny **plankton** that are found on the edges of the reef, but when a predator appears they dash for the shelter of the coral.

WHAT IS CORAL?

Corals are tiny, jelly-like animals with a hard outer "skeleton" made of calcium carbonate; the main material in limestone. They do not move around but live attached to rocks. When the coral itself dies the skeleton is left behind. New corals build on the skeletons of the old ones, and in this way the corals gradually build up into barriers and ridges in the sea.

Almost frozen

At the other extreme, a few fish are adapted to the cold of Antarctic seas, where the water is almost freezing. You might think that it is too cold to live here, but these fish have special chemicals which act as "antifreeze" in their blood to stop it turning to ice. Their blood is also clear because it has no red blood cells. The main job of red blood cells is to carry oxygen from the gills to all the cells of the body. Very cold water holds much more oxygen than warm water, however, so the fish do not need red blood cells.

The dark depths

In the deep ocean it is dark and cold, and there is little food. The huge pressure of the water at this depth would crush a human diver, but some fish are able to live here. Fish living in the ocean depths have adapted in many strange ways. The umbrella-mouth gulper is little more than an enormous mouth that can swallow food items bigger than itself, and a stomach that can expand to hold the food. Food is so scarce in the ocean depths that the gulper needs to be able to eat anything that comes along, no matter how big.

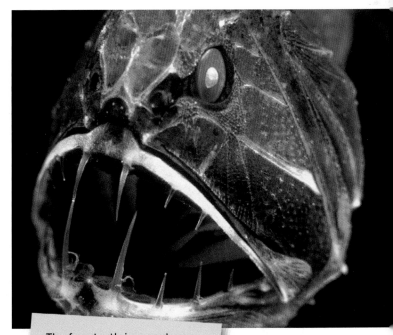

The fangtooth is an extreme deep water species that lives at depths of about 4,880 metres (16,000 feet). Food here is scarce, so the fangtooth will eat just about anything it can find.

Freshwater *fish*

More than ninety-nine per cent of all water on Earth is in the oceans, but only about sixty per cent of all species of fish live there. The rest live in fresh water. There are all kinds of habitats in fresh water from rushing mountain streams to still ponds.

Fast-running water

Fast-running water has more oxygen in it and is usually colder than the water in lakes and ponds. Trout, salmon, and grayling are all fish that generally live in fast-running water. They are active, fast-swimming fish. All animals need oxygen to get energy from their food. The high levels of oxygen in fast-running water allow these fish to move quickly to catch prey. They are also adapted to the cold temperatures. Some species of freshwater fish cannot survive if the water becomes too warm.

In very fast-flowing mountain streams, the current can be too strong for fish to swim against. Hillstream loaches are fish that have adapted to this situation by developing suckers on their fins, so that they can cling to rocks.

Channel catfish generally live in slow-moving water, in areas where the bottom is muddy but the water is clear. They hunt at night, using their barbels (feelers) to sense when prey comes near.

SURVIVING IN RIVERS AND SEAS

A few fish species have special adaptations so they can survive both in fresh water and in seawater. The bull shark is at home both in large rivers and lakes, and in the ocean. This allows it to hunt in freshwater rivers, where there are no other really large predators to compete with. In fresh water, the bull shark reduces the concentration of salts in its cells and produces large amounts of urine to stop itself from swelling up with water.

Lakes and ponds

Fish in slow-running or still water tend to be slower moving, because there is less oxygen in the water and so they cannot use as much energy. Fish that live in this kind of environment include carp and catfish. Both these groups of fish have sensitive barbels (feelers) around their mouths, which they use to feel for prey or food on the river bed.

Fresh water and sea water

Most ocean fish cannot survive in fresh water, and most freshwater fish cannot live in the sea. In both cases, the reason is to do with the **salts** in the fish's cells.

In seawater, there are more salts in the surrounding water than in the fish's cells. This means that water is constantly leaking out of the cells to try and dilute the surrounding water. Bony fish have adapted to this situation by constantly drinking seawater. They also produce very little urine. In freshwater fish the cells contain more salts than the water, so water is constantly seeping into the cells. Freshwater fish have adapted by reducing the amounts of salt in their body fluids and by producing large amounts of urine.

When salmon return to fresh water to breed, they have to swim up rivers that often contain waterfalls. Only the strongest salmon, that have the power to leap the falls, are able to reach the breeding grounds and reproduce.

Finding food

The best-known sharks are sleek predators. The great white shark, for instance, is one of the most fearsome hunters in the ocean. There are more than 350 different species of shark altogether, however, and not all of them are predators.

Whale sharks have wide, flat heads and very large mouths. This allows them to filter large amounts of water as they swim along.

Filter feeders

The three biggest sharks – whale sharks, basking sharks, and megamouth sharks – are all **filter feeders**. This means that they eat tiny plankton and other small creatures by taking huge mouthfuls of seawater and then filtering out the food items. The water is then pushed out through the gills.

All three species have huge mouths, to take in as much as possible in each gulp. A whale shark's mouth, for instance, can be 1.5 metres (5 feet) wide – big enough to fit a double bed! Bristly structures in the mouth, called gill rakers, trap food and stop it from sweeping out through the gills. Sharks that are filter feeders do not need to swim fast to catch their prey, so their bodies are not as streamlined as those of predatory sharks.

Seabed feeders

Angel sharks and carpet sharks are often flattened so that they can lie on the seabed unnoticed and **ambush** passing prey. They are also **camouflaged** so that they blend in with their surroundings. Most of the time these sharks lie motionless, but their muscles are adapted to have tremendous power – to allow them to suddenly explode off the seabed and grab their prey.

DIFFERENT WAYS OF FEEDING

Because sharks do not all feed in the same way, different shark species can have different **niches** in the same habitat. A whale shark may cruise through a coral reef hoovering up small creatures. Smaller sharks may hunt for food in the cracks and crevices of the reef, while bottom feeder sharks lie in wait on the seabed. Larger sharks hunt for bigger prey, including smaller sharks.

Different kinds of predator

The sharp-nosed, sleek shape of a "typical" predator shark helps it move quickly through the water when chasing prey. Different shark species hunt prey in different ways. Dogfish sharks get their name because they hunt in packs, like dogs or wolves. Mako and blue sharks rely on speed to chase down their prey. Great white sharks **stalk** their prey, and then suddenly strike.

Amazing senses

Predatory sharks have superb senses. They need them because finding prey in the huge ocean can be very difficult. Over long distances sharks rely on smell and hearing. Sharks can smell blood and other scents from several kilometres away. They can also hear low sounds especially well – the kind of sounds that prey make as they swim.

As a shark gets closer to its prey, other senses become important. Sharks can pick up pressure changes in the water, using a sense organ called the lateral line. Fish send out pressure waves through the water as they swim.

Most sharks have another unusual sense – they can pick up the tiny electric currents produced by an animal's nerves as it moves. At close range a shark can track prey by this sense alone.

Great white sharks are among the fiercest predators in the sea. Adults hunt large fish, including other sharks, as well as penguins, seals, porpoises, and dolphins.

Bony fish feeding

The basic source of food in the ocean is plankton, which is a collection of very tiny living things that drift through the water. Plankton includes many microscopic, plant-like creatures called algae, plus many tiny animals that are not big enough or strong enough to swim against the ocean currents. Plankton float where the ocean takes them.

All fish rely ultimately on plankton for food, however, different species feed on all kinds of other foods, from shellfish to sharks.

Plants and plankton

Parrotfish and some other species eat plant-like algae growing on coral reefs. Surgeonfish and some other species make algae "gardens" by clearing coral from an area to give the algae more space to grow. The fish feed on these gardens of algae, which grow much more quickly than in other parts of the reef. Many fish feed on seaweed, which is another kind of algae.

Many kinds of fish that live in large **schools**, such as herring, anchovies, and sardines, feed on plankton. Plankton feeders do not have to "catch" their food. Once they find a rich source of plankton they can just swim through it, eating as they go.

Anchovies and other schooling fish are important food for people. Millions of tonnes of anchovies and other schooling fish are caught each year.

Fish eat fish

Most fish are **carnivores**. They eat shellfish and other sea creatures, but most of all they eat other fish. Different species have adapted to use different methods for finding and catching food. Many kinds of fish are territorial. They live in a **territory** with at least one good source of food in it and defend this territory against other fish. Cichlids (freshwater fish such as angelfish) are an example of territorial fish.

Other fish are "sit-and-wait" predators. They stay in one place, waiting for prey to come close by. When the prey is near enough, the predator strikes.

Other predators are more active and seek out their prey. Large, open-ocean predators, such as tuna and barracuda, are known as **pelagic** fish. These fish travel long distances through the surface waters of the ocean. They feed on schooling fish, following the schools as they travel through the oceans. They usually hunt and feed in groups.

Scavenger fish

Some fish are **scavengers** – they eat the dead remains of fish and other creatures. Piranhas are a group of freshwater fish found in the rivers of South America. Piranhas have a reputation for attacking large animals in the water, but they often feed on dead and rotting meat. Their scavenging plays an important part in keeping the rivers clean.

ENERGY IN THE OCEANS

All energy in the oceans comes originally from the Sun. Algae in the plankton use the Sun's energy to make food, using a process called **photosynthesis**. This is the same process that land plants use to make their own food.

Animals in the plankton eat the algae, and then other sea creatures eat the plankton. The plankton-eaters are themselves eaten by predators. In this way, energy from the Sun spreads through ocean **food chains**.

The sicklefin lemon shark feeds on smaller sharks, rays, and other fish. It is found around reefs and in lagoons.

Unusual feeders

Some fish have very unusual ways of getting food. These fish can seem very strange to human eyes, but in the fierce competition for food and space, their unusual adaptations help them to survive.

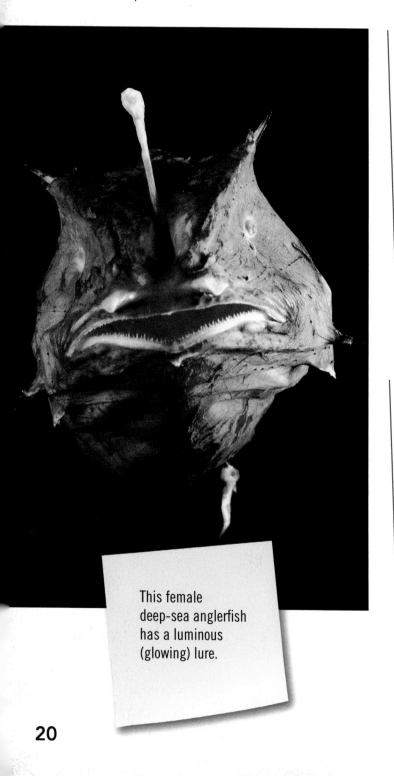

This female deep-sea anglerfish has a luminous (glowing) lure.

Deadly snipers

In freshwater habitats, many fish eat insects and other small creatures on the surface of a pond or other stretch of water. The archerfish has an adaptation that allows it to feed on insects that are beyond the reach of other fish. If it spots an insect sitting on a branch above the water, the archerfish fires a powerful jet of water from its mouth. If the jet hits the insect it tumbles into the water and the archerfish snaps it up. The archerfish can fire with great accuracy up to a distance of about 1.2 metres (4 feet).

Fishing tackle

When some fish go fishing, they literally use a rod and line. Anglerfishes are a group of about 300 species, all of which have developed a "lure" on their forehead. The lure is a dangling lump of flesh that attracts prey, like bait. The anglerfish lies on the seabed, completely still except for the dangling lure, until a small fish or other prey animal comes to investigate. Once it is close enough, the anglerfish opens its huge mouth quickly and sucks the victim in. Many anglerfish live in deep-sea habitats and have lures that glow in the dark.

Urchin turnover

Triggerfish are common in shallow tropical seas around the world. Several species of triggerfish can fire a jet of water like the archerfish. However, they use this ability in a very different way.

Sea urchins are common on coral reefs. Their long, poisonous spines make them almost impossible to attack, but they are not safe from triggerfish. The triggerfish fires a jet of water at the base of the sea urchin, knocking it over. The underside is not protected by spines, so the triggerfish can attack it there and eat it.

Mutual benefit

A few fish get their food through close association with other fishes. Cleaner wrasses feed on small parasites that live on the bodies and fins of larger fish. The wrasses "set up business" at a cleaner station, where fish that are suffering from parasites come to be cleaned. Often queues of fish wait their turn to get cleaned up by the wrasses.

SNEAKY MIMIC

The sabre-toothed mimic blenny looks remarkably similar to the cleaner wrasse that get rid of fish parasites, but the blenny is not interested in cleaning. Larger fish allow the blenny to get near, thinking it is a cleaner wrasse. Then they get a nasty shock as the blenny takes a bite out of them!

A potato cod is cleaned by two young hogfish, which also act as cleaner fish.

Shark camouflage

Camouflage is not just an adaptation to help prey to hide from predators. Predators also use camouflage to help them sneak up on their prey without being noticed.

The different shades of colour on a shark can be seen here.

Bland is good

A "typical" shark is a neutral grey, blueish, or brownish colour along its back. The colour shades into a much lighter, silvery grey on the underside. This bland colouring helps the shark to blend in with the general colour of the sea.

The shading of colour from light below to dark above is known as **countershading**. Many fish have this kind of countershading. It makes them more difficult to see from above or below. Looking down from above the ocean looks dark, so being darker coloured on top makes a shark less obvious. On the other hand, the ocean looks light when looking up towards the surface. A light belly helps a shark blend in with the lighter colours of the surface.

LIGHT CAMOUFLAGE

The Cookie-cutter shark is a small deep-sea shark, about 50 centimetres (20 inches) long. The Cookie-cutter camouflages itself with light. The shark's underside glows in the dark, which makes it difficult to see from below against the bright background of the ocean surface.

Spots and patterns

Not all sharks are plain-coloured. Dogfishes are mostly small sharks. Many are brown and grey, with patterns of spots on their bodies. Dogfishes live near the seabed, and the spots and patterns help to break up the outline of their bodies. Some species can even change colour – becoming lighter or darker to match the colour of the seabed.

Angel sharks are bottom-dwelling sharks that live in areas where the seabed is sandy. Their bodies are flattened, and their sandy colour with blotchy patterns blends in perfectly with the sandy seabed. Angel sharks lie half-buried in the sand and ambush small fish and squid as they pass.

Wobbegongs are found on coral reefs around Australia and south-east Asia. They are camouflaged with bold symmetrical patterns. When they lie among the corals, these patterns make them look like just another part of the reef. A fringe of skin flaps around the mouth and looks like pieces of coral, which helps to break up the shark's outline.

Wobbegongs rest by day, then ambush passing fish, crabs, and octopuses at night. Their camouflage is probably more important to keep them hidden while they are resting than for catching prey at night.

Wobbegongs belong to a group known as carpet sharks. Their superb camouflage makes them almost invisible. The skin around this shark's mouth looks like seaweed!

Camouflage in bony fish

Sharks use camouflage to help them get close to their prey, but camouflage can also help prey species to hide from their enemies. Bony fish use camouflage in all kinds of ways. Along the coasts of the north Atlantic, the sandy browns and greys of flatfish blend in with the sandy or gravelly seabeds where they live. Among the riot of colour of a coral reef, however, fish need to be boldly coloured and patterned to hide themselves.

Some fish have a limited ability to change colour but few are as good as the flatfish, which can change their colour within minutes. This flatfish has changed its colour to blend amazingly well with the sandy area it is lying on.

Blending in

Many kinds of bony fish are camouflaged to blend in with their surroundings. Bottom-dwelling species, such as toadfish, are camouflaged to blend in with the colours of the seabed. Flatfish, such as sole and plaice, have gone one step further with this kind of camouflage. They can change their colours and patterns to match the area they are lying on. A few small species, such as some gobies, have a transparent body, which really helps them blend in!

Some smaller fish have adapted their whole body shape to match with something in their environment. The pygmy seahorse looks exactly like the sea fan that it lives on (a sea fan is a kind of branching coral). It was only discovered accidentally by scientists studying the sea fan. Other examples include the freshwater leaf fish, which looks just like a dead leaf, and the sea dragon, which looks like a waving frond of seaweed.

Leafy sea dragons get their name from the leaf-like protusions all over their bodies. They also move very slowly in the water, resembling floating seaweed as they drift by.

Nose camouflage

Night hunters, such as sharks, eels, and other predators, do not use sight to find their prey – they most often use smell and sound. This is a real problem for daytime species, because night hunters can sniff them out while they are asleep. Some parrotfish have evolved a way to camouflage their smell from predators. At night, they sleep in a cocoon of mucus that they **secrete** around their bodies. The mucus makes it much harder for moray eels and other predators to smell the parrotfish.

STANDING OUT FROM THE CROWD

Some fish are not camouflaged – their bold colours and patterns make them stand out from their surroundings. Often this is a warning to predators that the fish is poisonous or tastes bad in some way. Some fish that are perfectly tasty have developed the same colours and patterns as a poisonous species. The mimic filefish, for example, looks very similar to an unrelated fish – the black-saddled puffer. Puffer fish are very poisonous and predators avoid eating them. They avoid eating the mimic filefish too, but only because it looks so similar to the puffer fish.

Shark defences

Sharks are not generally thought of as fish that have enemies. However, most sharks have a number of very dangerous enemies – other, larger sharks. Many species have evolved defences that give them a chance of escaping if they are attacked by a larger shark.

Horn sharks have large spines on their dorsal (back) fins. These spines make them an uncomfortable mouthful to eat.

Defence and attack

The adaptations that sharks use in hunting are also useful for defence. Open-ocean predators, such as blue and mako sharks, for instance, use their superb senses to give early warning of any enemies, and their speed to get away from trouble. Sharks such as angel sharks and wobbegongs rely on their camouflage to hide from predators as well as from their prey.

Thorny adaptations

Some sharks have adaptations that are definitely for defence rather than attack. Many dogfish sharks have spines along their backs that make them a painful mouthful to eat. Horn sharks also have long spines just in front of their dorsal (back) fin.

Bramble sharks would be even more unpleasant to eat – their whole body is covered in sharp, thorn-like denticles. They are also covered in a layer of sticky, horrible-smelling mucus. Together, these defences are enough to put off most predators!

LEFT HIGH AND DRY

Epaulette sharks need defences against a different kind of threat: lack of oxygen. These sharks live in shallow waters around coral reefs. At low tides they can find themselves in water very low in oxygen, or they may be left completely high and dry. To survive in this environment, epaulette sharks have an unusual adaptation. Scientists have found that they can shut down their body processes almost completely. This allows them to survive without oxygen for several hours.

Swell sharks

Swell sharks are fairly small sharks about 1 metre (3.3 feet) in length. They are slow-moving sharks that live on the seabed and ambush passing prey. When a swell shark feels threatened it bends itself round and grabs its tail in its mouth. It then sucks large amounts of water into its stomach, so that it swells to twice its normal size. Predators are put off by the increased size of the shark. This behaviour can serve another purpose. If a swell shark is hiding from predators in a rock crevice, swelling up makes it almost impossible to pull out of the crack.

Other defences

Whale sharks and other filter feeders are slow-moving and have no obvious defences against predators. Their main defence is their size. They are so enormous that few, if any, predators would risk an attack.

At the other extreme some small, bottom-feeding sharks have adapted to avoid predators through their behaviour. They feed at night, when fewer predators are active. During the day they find a hiding place where they can rest safely.

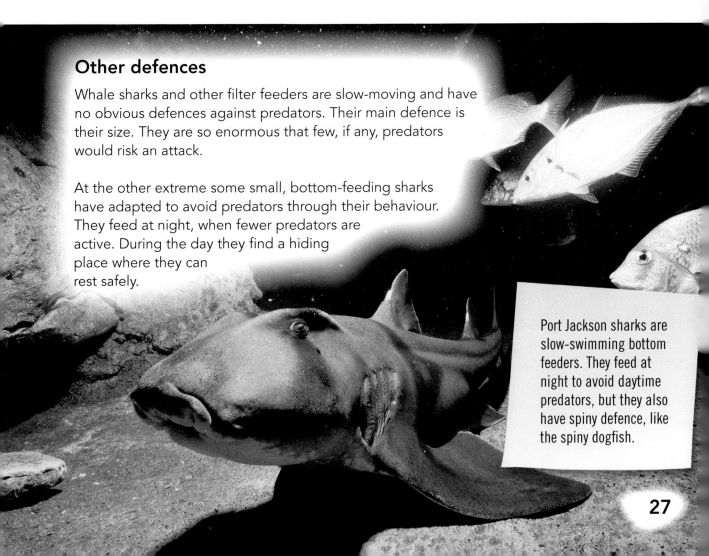

Port Jackson sharks are slow-swimming bottom feeders. They feed at night to avoid daytime predators, but they also have spiny defence, like the spiny dogfish.

Bony fish defences

All fish have some enemies. Survival is a constant battle between predators and their prey. As predators adapt to catch their prey, the prey develops adaptations to defend themselves.

By day, jackfish swim together in dense schools to avoid large predators, such as sharks and tuna. At night, the schools break up and the jackfish go hunting on their own.

Safety in numbers

One of the most common defences is for fish to gather in groups, or schools. A school may have only a few fish, or it may have millions. Gathering in large groups may not seem like a good way to avoid predators, but when fish gather in a tight group it is harder for a predator to pick out one fish to attack. If a predator does attack, the nearest fish scatter, and the confusing flashes of silvery bodies make it even harder for the predator to focus on individuals.

A group of garden eels feeding.

Other defences

Fish that do not live in schools have other methods of defence. Some fish protect themselves with armour. Garfish are long, thin fish with needle noses that live in rivers and along coasts. They have a tough skin and extremely hard scales. The scales have an inner bony layer, and an outer layer that is like the hard outer enamel layer of teeth. This "armour plating" is too tough for the teeth of most predators.

Other fish have spikes and spines on their body to make them difficult to eat. Often these spines are poisonous. The red lionfish looks very beautiful as it wafts through the water, but its long spines are deadly to most predators. Many other kinds of fish, including toadfish, scorpion fish, and stingrays, have poisonous spines. Probably the most poisonous, and certainly dangerous to humans, are stonefish. These superbly camouflaged fish dig themselves into the sand or mud of the seabed, making them almost impossible to spot. It is easy to tread on them by accident. The spines on the stonefish's back contain a strong poison that can be deadly if it is not treated quickly.

Hiding away

Another kind of defence against predators is to hide away. Camouflage is one form of hiding (see pages 24–25). In some habitats fish hide in cracks or gaps between rocks, while on sandy or muddy sea or river beds some fish dig burrows. Garden eels begin life as free-swimming larvae, but once they reach a certain size, they dig burrows in the sea bed where they stay for the rest of their lives. Groups of eels dig burrows close together, to form eel "gardens". They feed by extending the top half of their body out of the burrow and weaving their heads about in the water to catch plankton. If any danger threatens the eel quickly retreats into its burrow.

THE BIGGEST SCHOOLS

Atlantic herring are fairly small, silvery fish, up to 46 centimetres (18 inches) in length. A school of Atlantic herring can contain around 4 billion fish. This makes them the most numerous fish on Earth.

Unusual defences

In the struggle to survive, some fish have evolved very unusual ways to avoid predators. These range from puffing themselves up to flying through the air, and even using other creatures for protection.

A clownfish rests among the tentacles of a sea anemone. Clownfish feed on plankton and the leftovers of the anemone's food.

Puffers and porcupines

Puffer fish and porcupine fish are relatives of triggerfish. They are covered in poisonous spines like toadfish or stonefish. However, this is not their only defence against predators. When they feel threatened, puffer fish and porcupine fish suck in water and puff themselves out, like a swell shark. The combination of spines and a swollen body makes a very difficult mouthful for any predator.

Working together

Some fish have found ways to use other sea creatures for protection. Clownfish and anemone fish spend their lives among the poisonous stinging tentacles of **sea anemones**. However, they do not get stung and eaten by the anemones because they have a covering of special mucus that stops this from happening.

Medusafish and driftfish are two groups of fish that are often found swimming with jellyfish. Both live among the jellyfish's stinging tentacles. Like the clownfish, they are protected from stings by mucus coverings. They feed on the fish and other sea creatures that the jellyfish kills.

HITCHING A RIDE

Remoras get both protection and food by hitching a ride on sharks, large bony fish, or sea turtles. A remora has a large sucker on the top of its head, which it uses to attach itself to its "ride". The remoras feed on scraps that their hosts drop as they are feeding. Some species also feed on parasites attached to the larger fish's skin. Remoras have even been found inside a shark's mouth, acting as a living toothbrush! Even inside a shark's mouth the remora seems to be safe from being eaten, as no remora has ever been found in a shark's stomach.

Taking to the air

A few fish species escape from predators by taking to the air. Flying fish are a group of fish found in the surface waters of tropical seas. All flying fish have enlarged fins on the sides of their bodies that look like wings. Some species have just two "wings", while others have four.

When flying fish are chased by predators, they swim away at great speed, then leap into the air. In the air they spread their wing-like fins and glide. Predators cannot follow the flying fish into the air so they often lose track of their prey. Two-finned flying fish can glide up to 25 metres (80 feet), the length of a normal swimming pool, before landing in the ocean again. Four-finned flying fish can travel much further – up to 200 metres (650 feet) in one glide. To travel this far, the flying fish must reach speeds of 60 kilometres (37 miles) per hour before they take flight.

Despite their defences, flying fish are food for many predators, including tuna, marlin, porpoises, and many kinds of seabird.

Social sharks

Some sharks spend most of their time alone. Whale sharks and tiger sharks, for instance, live alone except when they are ready to reproduce. However, many kinds of shark are social animals. They live together and **migrate** in groups.

Pecking order

Every shark in a social group knows its place. Within any group of sharks there is a **hierarchy**, with some sharks being dominant over others. The position of a shark in this hierarchy is mostly decided by size – the largest sharks are highest in the "pecking order". There is rarely any fighting within a social group because each shark knows its own position.

A school of scalloped hammerhead sharks. In the summer, schools of scalloped hammerheads migrate towards the North and South Poles.

MATING CIRCLE

Scalloped hammerhead sharks hunt alone by night then gather together in groups during the day. The scalloped hammerheads also gather in large groups for mating. The females form a circle then the strongest females force their way to the centre. Males battle to get to the centre of the circle and mate with the strongest females. The strongest males make it to the centre and in this way the strongest pairs of sharks get to mate.

Migration

Like birds, many species of shark migrate in a regular pattern each year. Some sharks migrate in order to reproduce. Sandbar sharks spend the winter feeding around the coasts of Florida, USA. In early summer, they move north up the coast as far as Cape Cod, and produce their young in June. They then swim south again in September.

Other sharks migrate to follow their food. Basking sharks travel up to 3,400 kilometres (2,100 miles) each year, following the movements of the plankton that they feed on.

Eggs and babies

Most fish reproduce by external **fertilization**. This means that the females lay their eggs into the water and the males release their sperm over the eggs to fertilize them. However, only the most primitive sharks reproduce in this way. In most shark species, the male places his sperm inside the female. This adaptation means that the eggs are more likely to be fertilized, so female sharks do not need to produce as many eggs as most other fish do.

In some shark species the females lay eggs once they are fertilized. The eggs are protected inside a tough case, which is fastened to seaweed. The female leaves the eggs once she has laid them.

In most sharks, however, the young develop inside the female and are born as baby sharks. This adaptation gives the young a much better chance of survival.

Social life of bony fish

Bony fish live together in many different ways. Some species live alone, while others swim in schools of millions. Some species migrate long distances, while others stay in one place. Some fish lay millions of eggs, while others lay only a few. All of these differences are successful adaptations for survival and reproduction.

Feeding groups

How fish live depends largely on what they eat and how they eat it. Fish that feed on plankton can live in large groups because there is plenty of plankton for all individuals. Predators that hunt schooling fish can also live in groups because they also have an abundant food source. Some fish live in schools when they are younger, but live alone when they are fully grown. Barracudas and other large predators often live this way.

Fish such as flatfish and other ambush predators usually live alone. This is because they rely on surprise to catch their prey. With too many flatfish in one area, prey would be alerted and none of them would catch any food.

Every year, large numbers of salmon swim from the sea to their spawning grounds in rivers and pools. Once the salmon have spawned they die.

CHAMPION EGG LAYERS

Ocean sunfish are strange-shaped fish with large, broad bodies that end suddenly in a wide tail. When they spawn, female sunfish produce huge numbers of eggs. A single female can produce as many as 300 million tiny, floating eggs.

Long-distance travel

Most fish only reproduce at certain times of year and in particular places. Some species, such as eels or salmon, travel thousands of kilometres to **spawn** in the place where they themselves hatched. Salmon live most of their lives in the sea, then travel inland to spawn. Eels on the other hand live in fresh water, but travel to the sea to breed.

A female stickleback nests in the gravel on a stream bed. Her male partner is in the background.

Different groupings

Many kinds of fish gather together in huge groups to lay eggs and fertilize them. Schooling fish, such as anchovies and herrings, reproduce in this way. After spawning, the adults give the eggs no care. Each female has to produce thousands or even millions of eggs to ensure that at least some offspring survive long enough to grow up and mate.

Other fish species spawn in pairs and then lay eggs in nests. Sticklebacks, Siamese fighting fish, and butterfly fish all spawn in pairs. The males stake out a territory, which they defend from other males, and entice females to pair up with them. Some kinds of fish spawn in different groupings. In fish such as wrasses the males do not have territories. Instead, the strongest males gather a group of females around them and spawn with all the females in the group.

More on reproduction

In many bony fish species, eggs are abandoned once they have been fertilized, but this is not always the case. Some species go to great lengths to give their eggs a good start in life.

In sea horses and some species of pipefish, the males become "pregnant" with their eggs.

Caring for eggs

The amount of care fish give their eggs can vary greatly. Salmon, for instance, do little more than cover their eggs with a layer of gravel. Fish that pair up often look after their eggs once they have been laid. Male sticklebacks, for example, build a nest in their territory, where the female lays her eggs. The males then guard the eggs until they hatch. Species that nest and guard like this produce far fewer eggs, because each egg has a much better chance of survival.

Many species of cichlids (fish that live in the large lakes of east Africa) carry their eggs around. In these species, the female lays her eggs and then picks them up in her mouth. The male fertilizes them in her mouth and the female keeps them there until they hatch. Sometimes she may continue carrying the young fish for a time after hatching.

Among sea horses, it is the male that carries the eggs. The female lays her eggs into a pouch on the male's abdomen (stomach). The male carries the eggs in the pouch until they hatch.

Bitterlings have evolved a unique way to protect their eggs while they develop. The female bitterling has a long egg-laying tube that she uses to lay her eggs inside the shell of a freshwater mussel. The male sheds his sperm into the mussel. Safe from predators, the eggs develop inside the mussel for 2 or 3 weeks. When the young hatch they swim out of the mussel, leaving it unharmed.

Care after hatching

Once the eggs have hatched few fish care for them further. In sticklebacks, Siamese fighting fish, and a few other species, the males continue to defend the young for a short time after they have hatched.

SEX-CHANGE FISH

Humans are usually either male or female. This is true for most other vertebrates, but scientists have found that many fish species change sex during their lives. Fish born as males may later become females, and fish born as females may later become males. This often happens in groups with one dominant male and a group of females, such as groupers or seabass. If the dominant male dies one of the females will change sex to take his place.

In clownfish the opposite change happens. Clownfish live in small groups with a dominant female, instead of a dominant male. If the dominant female dies a male changes sex to take her place.

Coral groupers are neither permanently male nor permanently female — they can change sex. The change usually takes several days.

Sharks under threat

Sharks are fierce predators. The largest species, such as the great white, can occasionally be dangerous to humans, but humans are much more dangerous to sharks. **Top predators**, such as the great white and the mako shark, are endangered because of fishing and other human activities.

Many sharks are caught and killed accidentally by fishing boats. The numbers caught this way are very high. Tuna fishermen in the Atlantic Ocean accidentally catch over 500,000 sharks each year in their nets.

Sharks under attack

People kill sharks for many reasons. Some sharks are killed for food. In the United Kingdom, for instance, people eat a fish called rock salmon, which in fact is a kind of dogfish. Some sharks are also hunted for their skins. Once the scales have been removed, sharkskin makes very fine, tough leather. Sharks are also hunted for sport. Mako sharks are popular with sea anglers because they are very active when they are hooked, diving deep and leaping out of the water.

Sharks are also at risk from other human activities. Many of the millions of sharks killed each year are known as "by-catch" – this means sharks caught by accident when fishing for other kinds of fish. Many sharks are also killed in nets put around beaches to keep them out of areas where people are swimming. Pollution and building along coasts also affects some shark species, by destroying the places where they give birth to their young.

SHARK-FIN SOUP

Shark-fin soup is a dish originally from southern China, but it is now considered a delicacy by Chinese people around the world. As a result, shark fins can fetch high prices. Often fishermen that catch sharks simply cut off their fins and throw the rest back, leaving the shark to die slowly. Conservationists around the world are campaigning to end shark finning.

Slow to recover

Today, over 20 species of shark are under threat of **extinction**. Sharks such as the speartooth shark of Australia are seriously endangered, while nurse sharks, great whites, and whale sharks are also threatened. Most sharks grow slowly, mature late, and produce few young. This means that it takes time for shark numbers to recover. If too many sharks are killed the population will collapse dramatically.

Shark finning is banned in the United States and Australia. However, many fishing boats in these areas still fin sharks illegally. A single boat that was caught had fins from around 20,000 sharks.

Other threatened fish

Sharks are not the only fish under threat from human activities. Large modern fishing fleets are taking so many fish from the ocean that some kinds of food fish have disappeared in certain areas. Coral reefs are also under threat from global warming, pollution, and destructive fishing methods.

Overfishing

Schooling fish, such as cod, herring, and anchovies, have been important food fish for hundreds of years. However, today they have been **overfished**, and numbers have begun to fall. Some governments are now limiting the catches of certain fish to try and conserve them.

Coral reefs

About twenty-five per cent of the world's coral reefs have been destroyed in the last 30 years or so. Coral reefs are home to a third of all fish species, so reef destruction kills many kinds of fish.

Global warming is thought to be one cause behind the destruction of coral reefs. Coral reefs only survive within a narrow band of sea temperatures. General warming of the climate means that in some areas the sea is too hot for coral reefs to survive.

Clearance of forests on land and the use of **fertilizers** and **pesticides** in agriculture mean that many kinds of chemicals are polluting the water around coral reefs. This pollution is damaging the coral.

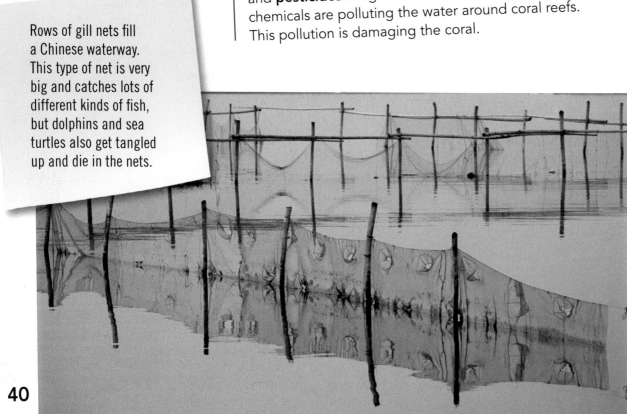

Rows of gill nets fill a Chinese waterway. This type of net is very big and catches lots of different kinds of fish, but dolphins and sea turtles also get tangled up and die in the nets.

When coral reefs are under stress, it can cause the corals to bleach, or turn white, like parts of the staghorn coral seen here.

Further damage

Much more obvious damage is caused by destructive fishing methods, such as blowing up areas of reef with explosives or pouring cyanide (a deadly poison) into the water. Both of these methods are illegal throughout south-east Asia, but they are still used regularly. These kinds of fishing cause complete destruction of areas of coral reef.

Millions of tourists visit coral reefs each year, sometimes causing damage to reefs. However, tourism plays an essential part in protecting coral reefs, because it is an important source of money. Local people want to preserve their reefs so that the tourists continue to come and visit.

LONGLINES AND GILL NETS

Two modern kinds of fishing cause great damage to fish populations because they kill many species besides those that they are designed to catch.

Longlines are enormous fishing lines up to 130 kilometres (81 miles) long, with thousands of hooks on them. They are a good way to catch many kinds of fish but they also catch other creatures such as dolphins, sharks, sea turtles, and seabirds. Gill nets are very fine but strong nets that can be up to 65 kilometres (40 miles) long.

Blasts from the past

The basic design of sharks has made them successful predators for over 375 million years. Today, there are only about 370 shark species, but there were many others in the past. Some sharks have survived while others have become extinct. Why is this?

The **fossilized** head of a hybodont: a prehistoric shark that lived during the Jurassic period (206 to 144 million years ago).

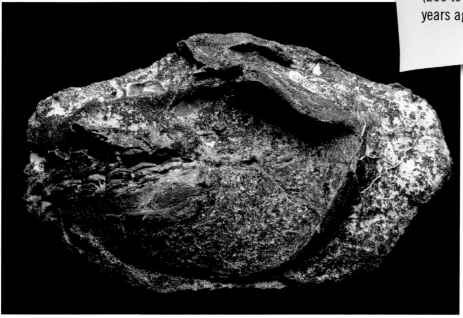

New, improved model

Some shark ancestors died out because the more modern fish that evolved from them were more competitive (better at finding food and surviving). Some of the earliest fish were fierce-looking predators with bony armour called placoderms. Placoderms appeared about 410 million years ago.

About 370 million years ago, the first shark-like predators, such as *Cladoselache*, appeared (see page 5). The light, cartilage skeleton and streamlined shape seems to have been a more successful adaptation, because by 360 million years ago most placoderms had died out.

Global disaster

Some shark ancestors were killed off in global disasters in the past. About 245 million years ago, an unknown catastrophe struck the Earth and killed off more than ninety-five per cent of all ocean life. This event is known as the Permian extinction. Many shark species died out in this period.

Loss of food

Another way that shark ancestors died out was through loss of their food source. About 24 million years ago, the Earth's climate became warmer and many new kinds of whale and other sea mammal began to evolve. One of these was an ancestor of the great white shark, called *Carcharodon megalodon*, which specialized in eating early whales. *Megalodon* lived in warm coastal waters and was a fierce, active predator. At 17 metres (55 feet) long (the length of about 1 and a half coaches) it was even bigger than a whale shark. Its mouth could open to about 2 metres (6 feet) wide – big enough to swallow a rhinoceros in one gulp. However, feeding such a huge shark took a lot of food. About 1.6 million years ago, some kinds of large whale died out, while others moved into cool, deep waters. *Megalodon* does not seem to have been able to adapt to the loss of its main food source, and this enormous shark became extinct.

A LIVING FOSSIL

In 1938, fishermen off the coast of South Africa caught a large, strange-looking fish. Because it looked so strange they took it to the local museum. After expert examination, the fish was discovered to be a coelacanth. This was a kind of fish that was thought to have died out 80 million years ago!

Modern survivors

Sharks such as the great white, the mako, and the blue shark are relatively new versions of a tried and tested design. Sharks survived the Permian extinction and the extinction 65 million years ago that killed off the dinosaurs. Today, they are under threat once more from the activities of humans. Whether sharks will survive this time may be decided by human activity.

These two teeth give an idea of the size of *Carcharodon megalodon*. The tooth on the left is the tooth of a great white shark, while the tooth on the right is from *Carcharodon*.

Further information

The 20 most endangered shark species

1. Ganges shark
2. Borneo shark
3. Basking shark – North Pacific & North-east Atlantic sub-populations
4. Speartooth shark
5. Whitefin Topeshark
6. Angular angel shark – Brazilian sub-population
7. Smoothback angel shark
8. Spinner shark – Northwest Atlantic sub-population
9. Pondicherry shark
10. Smoothtooth blacktip shark
11. Blacktip shark – North-west Atlantic sub-population
12. Dusky shark – North-west Atlantic & Gulf of Mexico sub-populations
13. Grey Nurse shark (also known as the Sand Tiger shark)
14. Great white shark
15. Gulper shark
16. Basking shark
17. School shark (also known as the Tope shark)
18. Blue-grey carpet shark
19. Porbeagle shark
20. Whale shark

Fish record-breakers

Biggest fish	Whale shark	12 m (40 ft.)
Smallest fish	Stout infant fish, Great Barrier Reef	7–8 mm (0.275–0.315 in.)
Fastest fish	Atlantic sailfish	110 km/h (68 mph.), over 100 m (328 ft.) in a leap
Most numerous fish	Atlantic herring	Schools of up to 4 billion individuals
Biggest predator	Great white shark	7 m (23 ft.)
Biggest ever fish	Leedsichthys	22 m (72 ft.)

Books

- Benchley, Peter (adapted by Karen Wojtyla). *Shark Life: True Stories about Sharks and the Sea* (Delacorte Press, 2005)
  – A book of true shark-stories written by the author of *Jaws*

- Fullick, Ann. *Life Processes: Adaptation and Competition* (Heinemann Library, 2006)
  – A look at how organisms have become uniquely suited to their environment

- Llewellyn, Claire. *My Best Book of Sharks* (Kingfisher Books, 2005)
  – A wealth of information about the deep-sea lives of this family of fascinating creatures

- MacQuitty, Miranda. *Eyewitness Guides: Shark* (DK Publishing, 2004)
  – An eyewitness guide to the world of some of the most awesome animals on the planet – their behaviours and their secret underwater lives

- Morgan, Sally. Animal Kingdom: Fish (Raintree, 2005)
  – Explores how and why animals are classified in specific groupings

- Solway, Andrew. *Wild Predators: Killer Fish* (Heinemann Library, 2005)
  – Explores the lives of killer fish and the deadly ways they hunt for prey

Websites

- BBC Science and Nature: Sea Life
  www.bbc.co.uk/nature/blueplanet/
  – BBC website on sea life, which includes articles on fish and other sea life, games, screensavers, and other goodies

- Nova World of Sharks
  www.pbs.org/wgbh/nova/sharks/world/
  – Articles and activities based upon the large number of different shark species found around the Cocos Islands off the coast of South America

- Yahooligans: Sharks
  search.yahooligans.yahoo.com/search/ligans?p=sharks
  – A list of websites about sharks

- Zoom Sharks
  www.enchantedlearning.com/subjects/sharks/
  – A simple, but informative, website on all sharks

Glossary

adaptation change that helps a living thing fit into its environment

algae tiny plant-like living things. Seaweeds are an example of algae.

ambush make a surprise attack from hiding

camouflage colour and patterning that help an animal to hide from its enemies

carnivore animal that eats meat

cartilage tough, springy material that makes up shark skeletons

cell tiny building block of all living things

coral small, tube-shaped animals with a hard, chalky "shell" that live attached to rocks

coral reef rocky ridges in warm, shallow seas that are covered with corals and many other forms of life

countershading colouring that makes an animal's body look flat and less obvious

dense substance that is closely compacted, making it heavy for its size

denticles tiny, triangular scales that look like teeth

direct competition when two species of living things live in the same habitat and eat the same foods. Eventually one species will dominate and the other will become extinct.

evolution process by which life on Earth has developed and changed

evolve develop gradually over a long period of time

extinction when all the individuals of a species has died out

fertilization process of a sperm cell combining with an egg cell to form the first cell of a new living thing

fertilizer natural material or chemical that is added to soil to make it better for growing plants

filter feeder animal that gets food by straining small creatures or tiny pieces of food from water

food chain series of plants and animals, each of which is food for the next

fossilized preserved animal or plant which has become a fossil

gamete male or female sex cell, usually sperm or eggs

gill breathing organs of a fish

habitat place where an animal lives

hierarchy organization of a group of animals into an order, where some animals are dominant over others

mate animal's breeding partner; also, when a male and female animal come together to produce young

migrate travel long distances each year from a summer breeding area to a winter feeding ground (area of the ocean where a group of fish go to feed every year)

niche particular place and way of life of one individual species within a habitat

over-fishing catching so many fish that the overall number of that fish species cannot recover and the species numbers decline

parasite living thing that lives and feeds on or inside another living thing

pelagic fish or other sea creature that lives in the open ocean

pesticide chemical that is used to kill insects, spiders, or other small creatures that feed on farm crops

photosynthesis process by which plants and algae use energy from the Sun, water from the soil, and carbon dioxide from the air to make their own food

plankton microscopic and very small living things that drift with the ocean currents

predator animal that hunts and eats other animals

pressure pushing or squeezing force

prey animal that is eaten by a predator

range places where a living thing is known to live

reproduce produce offspring

salts simple chemicals such as common salt (sodium chloride)

scavenge search for dead and rotting animals as food

scavenger animal that feeds on dead and rotting animals or other kinds of waste

school large group of fish or sea mammals

sea anemone sea creature that has a tube-shaped body topped by a mouth surrounded by stinging tentacles, which lives attached to the sea floor on coral reefs and in other places

secrete produce a liquid from a special part of the body known as a gland

spawn mate and lay eggs

specialized when a living thing is adapted to a particular habitat

species group of very similar animals that can breed together to produce healthy offspring

stalk hunt by slowly creeping up on prey

territory area that animals defend against other animals of the same species

top predator predator at the top of the food chain, that is not the prey of another animal

variation differences between individuals within a species

vertebrate animal with a backbone

Index